Introduction

November 26

"Let us go over to Bethlehem and see this thing that has happened, which the Lord has made known to us." And they went with haste and found Mary and Joseph, and the baby lying in a manger. - Luke 2:15-16

They return every year. The pilgrims arrive at our home on November 1, just like the swallows that return to Capistrano in March 19. They stay for about a month. They are accompanied by a larger turkey than they themselves. It's like a scene from A Jurassic Park Thanksgiving when they stand too close together. Although he's carrying a small ceramic musket, it won't be large enough to take down the turkey. Her white ceramic apron is ready to cook any ceramic game he brings back from the hunt. If her pilgrim man meets this turkeysaurus, he will not bring home the turkey.

As most Americans, I associate pilgrimage with the Mayflower and Plymouth Rock. The word pilgrim was used long before the brave men and women who arrived at Cape Cod's grassy sand dunes on November 9, 1620.

Because of their actions, they were pilgrims. They were pilgrims on a journey with an underlying spiritual purpose. The pilgrims who traveled to America, just like Chaucer's group in The Canterbury Tales, Bunyan's Pilgrim in Pilgrim's Progress and the ancient Israelites who made the pilgrimage to Jerusalem each year, were motivated by a spiritual purpose.

Pilgrims have been a part of American folklore and history for centuries. This book is about Christmas pilgrims, not the pilgrims who travel to Bethlehem each December to see Jesus' birthplace on the traditional anniversary. Instead, I invite to you to become a Christmas Pilgrim along with me on the journey of your mind and heart to Bethlehem. As we travel towards our destination, I will share my stories.

You will hear stories from other pilgrims about their experiences and the impact it had on their lives.

You and the shepherds who are running frantically during Christmas can have a lot in common. You are probably also in a rush. They weren't late to the holiday party, or hurrying to get their Christmas gifts delivered by the deadline. They weren't hurrying to get to the mall or the post office. They were speeding to Bethlehem. I ask you to let go of all the hurries and join them on this journey. For the next 30 days, I ask you to take a few minutes each day to stop and reflect on the experiences of the shepherds as well as the other pilgrims when they arrived in Bethlehem.

I hope that you will accept my invitation to join me on this journey. I hope you will see some of the most sacred wonders. I believe you will be forever changed. To make this journey as personal as possible, you will be called Pilgrim. That is fine with me.◆◆◆

November 27

Mary, Joseph, the Magi, and the shepherds were all called from their homes and places to be taken to Bethlehem to witness the birth of Jesus. Although they didn't know the meaning of Christmas, they responded to the call through angels, stars, and soldiers to travel to the city. The Christmas experience changed the lives of these original Pilgrims.

What does this mean for you? Are you being called to escape the pressures and busyness of Christmas? To experience the truth about Jesus' birth? Have you been changed by the fact that Jesus came into this world?

It is difficult to understand and see the meaning of Jesus' birth in hurry or with a crowd. Our hurry-up, do more, filled-to-overflowing days are incompatible with contemplation and reflection. Only in stillness, calm, and silence can we discover truth and see how it affects us.

Are you finding that modern life's hectic pace is detrimental to your spiritual well-being? It seems impossible to spend quality, daily time with God because we are so busy. All of us sing the same refrain "I don't have time." We may have to admit that a busy schedule can make it difficult to cultivate a spiritual life.

It can be difficult to find a quiet place for a while. Some people are more comfortable in crowds than others. No matter what your reactions to being in a crowd, few people are able to spend much time alone. People with whom we live or work can be channel of God's blessings, but they can also hinder the intended blessings. The wise pilgrim is aware that he needs companionship along his journey as well as solitude.

This pilgrimage is a lonely one. It is a deeply personal decision to go to

Bethlehem to see the manger. Jesus' birth is one thing. The impact that this fact has on your life and daily activities is another. It doesn't suffice to understand how Bethlehem's events impacted the world, or how the birth occurred.

The impact of the baby on others was profound. The Christmas Pilgrims should also consider how Mary's baby may have a personal impact on them.◆◆◆

November 28

Yes, Pilgrim. You and I need to be "called away" in Christmas. I don't know who or what may be your messenger calling you to come. It won't likely be a Roman soldier and it probably won't even be an angel. It could be a song, or a sermon. This little book might be it. If you do hear it, please answer the call. You will be forever changed if you answer the phone.

To learn more about God's power and faithfulness, you must be called away. These matters can be easily understood on an intellectual level but completely ignore their effect on your life. This will help you understand these concepts in your own heart.

It will be worth making small changes to your daily routine to allow for some personal reflection. When we apply these lessons to our lives, we find the key to releasing ourselves from the prison of doubts, worries and fears.

How can you deal with your empty loneliness and gnawing guilt better than to look into the manger-cradle? See the one whose names are "Savior" or "God with Us?" Do doubts and skepticism have you becoming so unsure of yourself that you no longer trust anyone? It would be like cleaning out a stained, dirty window to see the reminder in flesh that God keeps all promises.

Do our hearts yearn for assurance of love, even when we realize how unlovable and stifling we are? This pilgrimage is for you if you feel that your worship is too rigid and repetitive, or if your spiritual awareness is limiting,◆◆◆

Mary

November 29

In those days a decree went out from Caesar Augustus that all the world should be registered.
- Luke 2:1

As they entered the village's central market square, the soldiers' body armor creaked. As they waited for the crowd to arrive, their shields and helmets reflected the sunlight. Their battle gear was not worn by them to be threatened by the peasants but rather as a subtle reminder that Rome has power over her subjects.

Palestine was an outpost of the great empire. There was no glory in their current assignment. They were messenger boys and couriers on this tour through the dusty Galilee towns. The rank soldier reached into his pack and pulled out a scroll. The scroll was unfastened by the leather strap, which he untied.

He did the same thing in the previous poor village. Now he read the decree. They understood that the census was intended to establish tax rolls. The imperial messenger said: "Most excellent Quirinius is your benevolent Governor, and orders all Jewish subjects report to their ancestral homes for registration."

As the words of the decree were spoken, the murmur turned into a commotion. They couldn't pay more taxes. It was difficult. They couldn't travel without being dangerous and difficult. Some of the most religious citizens prayed silently to God for the salvation of their oppressors.

Mary was on her way back from the market with some food when the announcement came to her. Walking became easier for her as she grew in pregnancy.

It was difficult. Just a few months after the baby was born, Joseph and she were informed that they would need to travel 90 miles to Judea to take part in the tax census. She understood the frustration of her neighbors. As the baby moved inside her, she instinctively held onto the basket with one hand. She smiled quietly as God led her to the place Micah had predicted for her baby's birth hundreds of years ago.

Pilgrim: Can you imagine a way God might be working in the difficult situation you are facing right now? You can trust that God is working in this situation even though you don't know how. Ask God for a faith that is like Mary's.◆◆◆

November 30

"Behold, I am the servant of the Lord; let it be to me according to your word." - Luke 1:38

The way we view the journey to Bethlehem will depend on our understanding of why we are there. It was a matter for soldiers to announce the plans to Nazareth residents. They had to give the orders and Rome's subjects had to follow their lead.

Do you remember obeying orders out of obligation? Did you ever complete a task or follow a directive out of obligation? It is embarrassing to admit that there have been times when I was unable to enjoy the task or had no joy. We can sympathize with those who cheat themselves and others who do not perform spiritual work for the purpose of serving God.

Pilgrim, I hope that you begin this journey to Bethlehem with hope and not despair. I can't force you to go along, but I will not let the page slide by. I can only invite and promise that you will enjoy the journey. If daily reading and pondering becomes a burdensome task in your mind, you could miss the point.

I want to rekindle your appreciation and awe for Bethlehem. Resentment at having to follow my lead will not allow you to experience the wonder and worship that I want. We sometimes feel like a child who is forced to go visit family members when they would prefer to stay at home. This can lead us to pout and miss out on some truly wonderful experiences.

It is unlikely that there was joy in Judea and Galilee as the news about the census spread. However, I can only imagine that one heart heard and was received

The announcement contained a completely different message. Mary's life was full of interesting events over the last few months. When the angel appeared, she was only twenty-one years old and was engaged. Although she was innocent, she knew enough to be certain that she couldn't possibly become pregnant. She listened to the angel explain how it would happen and accepted her place in the plan. "Behold, my servant is the Lord; let it happen to me according to Your word," Pilgrim's submission to God's will is the key to her story and ours.

What would you say about the difference between obeying out of duty and submitting because of trust? Which is more typical of your relationship to God?

December 1

“Behold, I am the servant of the Lord; let it be to me according to your word.” - Luke 1:38

Do you mind focusing with me for a few more days on Mary's words Amazing display of servant-hearted, unconditional surrender! Although some of my "surrenderings" have been unconditional, I must admit that they were not always. What about you? Do you remember feeling complete surrender to your life and God's will?

I think we are robbed of a blessing when escape clauses and exceptions are added to our surrender to God. Like me, Pilgrim I can imagine you've done this - even though genuine surrender reduces stress and frustration around obedience. We are blessed with peace that can endure any difficult situation and overcome all obstacles when we trust God's plan for our lives, no matter what it may be.

This doesn't mean that there won't be difficult circumstances and obstacles. It is not possible to imagine Mary's life in the wake of the angel's announcement. Imagine telling Joseph.

"Honey, I'm going have a baby!"

"Yes, dear, if God blesses us with children, we will be so happy." "I can't wait."

"No, you don't understand. I am pregnant. Right now. "I am going to have my baby."

"But that's impossible!" Joseph's face became a maze of emotions as incredulity was transformed into doubt, doubt to suspicion, suspicion to hurt, hurt to anger, and suspicion to suspicion.

"Let me explain! I was contacted by an angel. He said that I would have a baby. The baby is the Son Of God!" She had experienced it many times.

Although we rehearsed the story, it was still difficult to believe. (Reality check) Would you believe your daughter if you told her such a story if you were a father? Would you believe your daughter's story if you were a mother? Would you expect your fiancée to believe a story such as this if you were engaged? This story is something we have learned from Sunday School. It is in the Bible. Mary was forced to tell Joseph that they were not in Sunday School, and that it wasn't in her Bible. Mary would have been divorced if the angel hadn't also confirmed her story to Joseph.

It may seem that God's will seems demanding or difficult to you. But, Mary's selfless spirit during the events that led to her pilgrimage to Bethlehem is a testament to that. You will be amazed at her incredible surrender.

Is it possible that following God's will has caused friction in your relationships? What can you do to relieve tension when making big decisions?◆◆◆

December 2

"You are blessed, because you believed the Lord would do what he said." - Luke 1:45, NLT

Mary was eager to get up and head for the hills. Elizabeth was her only hope. The evidence of the angel's words would be evident in Elizabeth's old relative's large belly. She was able to make sense of the angel's words about Elizabeth's pregnancy when she saw her, just like the angel said.

She arrived in the Judean hill county, where Zechariah was living with Elizabeth. Dr. Luke relates that Elizabeth's baby leapt from her womb at Mary's voice, and that Elizabeth was filled the Holy Spirit. This is how the Spirit refers to how an old woman mysteriously pregnant became the first person in the story to call Mary's baby "Lord." She also told her young visitor about how she felt honored that Mary had come to visit her and how the baby within her leaping for joy when Mary spoke.

All this confirmed for Mary the message of the angel a few days earlier. Did Mary at this point tell anyone about the angel's message to her? She had pondered how she would explain it and who would believe it. Elizabeth was already celebrating and knew everything about it before she could tell her!

Mary heard an interesting comment from Elizabeth about Elizabeth's blessings. She stated, "You are blessed because you believed the Lord would do what He said." This line is great for Christmas Pilgrims such as you and me. It is the culmination of Abraham's journey through the Old Testament. It summarises the gospel and explains in simple terms how God's good news works.

It is possible for a scheme of redemption to work. This is how the thousands of people who received the good news from Acts were saved. It is the foundation for the new hope and changed lives of the disciples who received the letters that we now call the epistles of the New Testament.

Pilgrims, it is important to understand the implications of this statement for us as we travel our own paths. It is about believing that God did exactly what he promised to do regarding the baby in Mary's womb becoming the Son of God. We also need to believe in God's ability to fulfill the promises he made about our lives.

Remember a time when God promised you a blessing and you did so. Give thanks!

Is there any promise God made that you have to trust God more in order to receive a blessing?

December 3

"You are blessed, because you believed the Lord would do what he said." - Luke 1:45, NLT

Let's not forget about this verse, which so beautifully demonstrates the relationship between trusting God and being blessed by Him.

A few years back, I created a small devotional book that contained fifty promises from the Bible and an application to your life. We printed it and bound it in church offices with a few volunteers. It was shared with us over a period of fifty days to strengthen our faith. We listened to and meditated on God's promises, from the promise of salvation in Jesus' name, to the promise God would be our father, to the promise that God would work in, on, and through us. He will provide for your needs; he'll give you wisdom and he won't leave you. He will protect your heart, give you rest, and give you eternal live. This list could go on. Even though I didn't refer to today's text in the little book, we realized more and more what Elizabeth meant. We are truly blessed when we believe that God will do what he said.

Believe me Pilgrim, we are blessed when God is trusted. This blessing could be joy at the solution of the most difficult problem in your life. This blessing could be found in the peace that we feel when we pray rather than worry. It may be confidence in facing whatever is thrown at us because we know he is there, just like David once said, "I will not fear any evil, for your are with me."

Christmas Pilgrims have this to be sure: God will bless us if we examine the promises of God, reflect upon what they mean, and embrace them with trusting faith. We will then feel joy at being heirs to the promises God made to Abraham long ago. God is trustworthy. God doesn't lie.

Pilgrim, God is trustworthy and will not lie to you.

tells you. Mary and you will be blessed because of your faith.

It is sometimes hard to believe a promise. Is there a promise God made that is particularly meaningful to you?

December 4

"My soul magnifies the Lord, and my spirit rejoices in God my Savior." - Luke 1:46-47

Some religions offer hope that humans can become God. Christianity is centered around the idea of God becoming one of us through Jesus Christ. The events surrounding Jesus' birth are the most important focus of the mystery of Incarnation.

The gospel is a belief that God created a baby in Mary's womb, without the intervention of a human father. The belief in God, the Creator of the world, opens the door to believing that God can cause a virgin child to be borne. If God created the original human beings, as Genesis says, then allowing a baby to grow in a woman's body without the help of a father should not be difficult. We can still sympathize with Mary who asked "How could this be?" The angel answered her question, and it should be enough to satisfy us: "For nothing is impossible with God."

The Magnificat (or Mary's Song) is a beautiful expression of worship and devotion to God. It is rooted in Scripture. Mary believed the prophecies. Her sense of wonder and adoration grew as she began to see the work of God in her life and how her place was in it.

You and I should be filled with wonder and praise when we see Jesus Christ in Bethlehem. The paradox of the Creator sleeping on a straw bed wrapped in cloth makes our minds reel. He is now in the manger, the one who created the plants that made his bed and his bedclothes. It is like the confusing images of mirrors reflecting in parallel mirrors. It is amazing to think of a mother giving birth and the baby who gave her her life. Faith takes over when understanding fails and accepts what it can't figure out.

The story of the baby in the manger is a reminder of just how far God would go to bring us back. God sent Jesus to die for us when sin entered the world, and all of humanity was separated from their creators. Jesus had to be born among us in order to die for us.

Trust is only tested when we are unable to understand why or want something completely different from what God has given us. These "trust tests" can be applied to your life.

December 5

And Mary said to the angel, "How will this be, since I am a virgin?" - Luke 1:34

Joseph was able to accept the amazing news from Mary and proceeded with the wedding. He also refused the privilege and pleasure of being with his spouse until the birth of the baby. Mary was not only subject to Joseph's judgment. The family and neighbors of Nazareth soon learned the truth. Mary was forced to take on the public opinion burden as her baby grew in her womb. It is unlikely that people were any different from today. It was probably unpleasant to go to either the market or the synagogue because of the whispered gossip.

Mary persevered despite hardship. The Roman decree was the way God would keep His promises to Abraham, David, and Mary. It would also allow for the fulfillment of the prophetic detail about Messiah being born in Bethlehem. Mary understood God's intention in sending her to Bethlehem even if everyone in the town didn't like the orders.

To be able to walk with God is essential. Are you able to trust that God is in control of all aspects of your life, including the difficult and unpleasant ones? Mary knew this because she was faithful during a difficult time in her life. This was not her fault. We can believe God is sovereign and accept that he can use our lives to fulfill his purposes, even if they are not ours.

Paul, the apostle, said that "We walk by faith not by sight." Do we filter news through our faith that God sees, loves and knows us? Are you able to trust that God wants the best for you? There are many counselors

Philosophers have observed that while we cannot control the events of life, we can manage our responses to them. People of faith should find this most true. Anxiety is a sign that we are worried about the future, how people will react and what we will do. I am probably low in faith if I worry.

As Christmas Pilgrims on our journey to Bethlehem I hope that we will be more dependent upon a God who is completely reliable. As Mary, I believe we will be able to see God's hand at work even when people around us are denying God or indifferent. Like the young woman who was chosen to become the mother of our Lord's Son, I pray that our hearts and wills will be dedicated to God's purpose and plans.

Think back to a time you were anxious about the unknown. What makes trust different from knowledge?

Joseph

December 6

And Joseph also went up from Galilee, from the town of Nazareth, to Judea, to the city of David, which is called Bethlehem, because he was of the house and lineage of David, to be registered with Mary, his betrothed, who was with child. - Luke 2:4-5

Joseph lived a normal life before becoming a Bethlehem bound pilgrim. He was already settled in Nazareth. He also had a family tree. It is difficult to trace our family's history beyond three to four generations today. Joseph and his family knew from a primitive time that there were no online records or genealogy software to help them find their family's genealogy. This heritage ties him to the story and pilgrimage as Joseph is traveling to Bethlehem because he is from this tribe, clan, and family.

These verses also hint at Joseph's future. The quiet carpenter had not only a past but also a plan for his future. Mary, his wife of ten years, was his commitment. They were married. Joseph and Mary were more than engaged. They were legally sworn to marry. They had many dreams and plans. They had already overcome the shock at the news of Mary's pregnancy. They would travel to Bethlehem in order to obey the Roman's decree. They would have a baby and then they could continue their lives together. The journey to Bethlehem, and the events that would take place there, would define their lives.

These verses remind us of how our pilgrimage fits in the context and meaning of life. We, like Joseph, have a past and a story. The novelist refers to a backstory, which is a history of events that have shaped and brought us to this moment. Aren't there hopes and dreams for the future? What will it take to make this journey?

Bethlehem change us?

Jesus came to Bethlehem in order to heal our past. All of us have done and said things that we don't like to think about. As we reflect on the mistakes we have made, shame and embarrassment rise up in us. Guilt can gnaw at those who have made mistakes that have left scars on their innocent conscience. All of these reasons, and more, are the main reasons why the Savior was born to remove guilt.

Jesus came to Bethlehem in order to give us hope and dreams, not fear and dread. Nobody who embarks on this journey should feel defeated. The pain of emptyness and frustration of brokenness are not the only things that Christmas Pilgrims must experience when they come to the manger. When we trust the promises made by the One who was born in Bethlehem, we find strength to face the future. You can change your perspective by understanding how precious you are to the Father who sent His Son. Our futures will be dramatically changed if we follow his example and go from Bethlehem.

Pilgrims need to understand that the here-and-now journey cannot be separated from its history and the legacy that follows it. That sounds like a curse without Jesus. We would be helpless victims of our own choices and fates if we didn't have his power to save and transform us. Jesus is able to release us from our past and promise the resources of heaven to ensure our future.

It is not necessary to allow worry about tomorrow or yesterday to steal our present. Stories about time travel are popular because they show how limited we are in our present. Is it not possible to go back and change a decision that has influenced your life? Every daydreamer imagines the future. The only person who can make any changes to the past or future is the Bethlehem baby.

Are you plagued by guilt or memories? What can Jesus do to help?

Do you worry about the future? What can we do to overcome our anxiety by having strong faith in God?

◆◆◆

December 7

"Is not this the carpenter's son?" - Matthew 13:55

Joseph, like the wise men is covered in mystery. An angel gave Joseph directions and suggested what to do. We know his father's and grandfather's names from the genealogy. We know that he was a carpenter (literally, tekton or stone mason). We don't know what he said, but the Bible says nothing. We don't know when or how he died but we assume he died before Jesus began his public ministry.

It is odd that so little information exists about the man God chose as his father figure in Jesus's life. It would be reasonable to expect that we would have more information on such an important character in the tale. He wasn't Jesus' father so the gospel writers don't give much detail about him.

Joseph, I believe, must have been involved with Jesus' development and training as a young child. Joseph must have taught Jesus his trade. It must have seemed a bit ironic. What is a carpenter to do with the Creator of the Universe? From what we know about Mary's husband I believe Jesus saw in Joseph a good example both of self-denial as well as godliness.

This Joseph was like another Joseph from the book Genesis. He was a dreamer. Three times, the angel of the Lord appeared in a dream to Joseph, telling him to marry Mary and to flee Egypt to escape Herod's death. An angel appeared to Joseph in a dream and convinced him that Mary's child was the Son of God. Joseph did exactly what the angel of God told him to do each time.

Dreams are not something I know much about. The only ones I can remember are those that I don't want to become a reality. But I do know that God did use them.

To communicate with the past, dreams can be used. This is another way God chooses to communicate through the ages.

What number of generations do you know or remember from your family? Are you a parent? Grandparents? Are there great-grandparents? Who was the most influential in shaping your early life and your values?
◆◆◆

December 8

And when the time came for their purification according to the Law of Moses, they brought him up to Jerusalem to present him to the Lord. - Luke 2:22

The best lesson Christmas Pilgrims can learn from this quiet, mysterious man? To listen to God and follow his lead. It is tempting to think, "If God spoke to me in dream, I would do whatever God told me." Are we listening to what he's already said?

Joseph listened to God, and he followed the instructions sent through other channels. Luke says that Jesus' trips to Jerusalem to circumcise him and then to present him as the firstborn in the temple were made "according to the Law of Moses" and "as written in the Law of the Lord." Joseph, Mary and Mary understood God's word and were following it.

We must not consider all obedience teachings as "legalistic." It is not about doing God's will. Legalism is a belief in law-keeping as the foundation of righteousness. It binds human opinion to dogma, as if man-made laws were God's words.

Joseph's faith in God shines through his humble obedience. My life should have demonstrated more of my trust. Pilgrim, I wonder if you feel the same about yourself.

Jesus said, "If I love you, you will follow my commands." Have you ever been hurt or betrayed by someone who claimed they loved you but did not care about you? Paul describes how love behaves in 1 Corinthians 13 and not how it feels. Love isn't just something you profess. Love is demonstrated in everything we do every day. It shows if we love ourselves more that we love Jesus. It shows in our actions, character, and conduct when we love the world or sinful pleasures or the acceptance of others more than God.

If we don't heed Jesus' words and follow his example, are we truly disciples of Jesus? Learning from Jesus and following his example is about becoming like him and expressing his will in our lives. John wrote that "We know we have come to love him if we follow his commands" and "Whoever claims he lives in him must live as Jesus did." Paul stated that he was crucified with Christ, meaning that he no longer lived but Christ lived in Paul. He was doing the same thing Jesus instructed disciples to do: deny yourself, take up your cross daily and follow Christ.

We know little about Joseph's childhood, but it is clear that he was faithful. He followed his obedience on his pilgrimage from Jerusalem to Bethlehem. If we truly want to know and see the Lord, then we must also obey him. Obeying the Lord will not be a badge of our accomplishments or a way to compare ourselves with fellow pilgrims. We can feel the joy of following Jesus' instructions and show our faith by doing what he asks Why is obedience so closely linked to faith and love as outlined in the Bible?

Are all obedience and teaching about obedience "legalism"?

December 9

When Joseph woke from sleep, he did as the angel of the Lord commanded him: he took his wife, but knew her not until she had given birth to a son. And he called his name Jesus. - Matthew 1:24-25

We are shown another aspect of Joseph's selflessness in the few words we hear about him in the gospel. What I do is displeases God because of my selfishness. Pilgrim, have you ever noticed this about yourself? How many crimes, abuses, and wars that are reported daily in the news are caused by selfishness? Matthew states that Joseph brought Mary home to be his wife when the angel mentioned the baby. But he did not have a union with Mary until the birth of Jesus. Later, Jesus was a young man who began his ministry. His hometown people were shocked by him and asked: "Isn't this the carpenter's son?" Isn't Mary his mother's maiden name? "Are his brothers and sisters not here with us?" This indicates that Joseph was married to Mary and had a normal marriage after Jesus' birth. Joseph was not legally married, but he did not have the joy of being with Mary before Jesus' birth.

She.

According to popular culture, sex is like water or air. You can't live without it. Some people believe it is unreasonable to expect young men to stop having sexual relations with their partners until they get married. One man or woman may choose to be single and chaste and become the subject of gossip and suspicion. Many married couples have used the inability of their spouse to have sex due pregnancy or illness to break their vows.

Contrary to all this, Joseph refused to be united with his wife until Jesus was born. It was selfless.

Christmas is a time to show our selflessness and selfishness. Do you recall litmus paper from the science lab? It tells you whether the substance is stable.

Acids and bases can change the color of a substance if they come in contact with it. Perhaps the wrapping paper that we place under Christmas trees is litmus paper. Do we get more joy from the presents we open and then unwrap? Or the ones we give and wrap? Our hearts may be self-giving or selfish depending on how we give and get.

It is normal for children to get excited about Christmas presents. As parents and grandparents, it's normal for kids to be excited about the gifts we give. It's thrilling to see a child learn the grace of giving.

Do you remember a gift that you were more excited to give than receive?

Who did you give it to and why was it so rewarding?

Have you ever met someone who has shown selflessness and love? What can you do to follow their example?

The Angels

December 10

And the angel said to them, "Fear not, for behold, I bring you good news of great joy that will be for all the people." - Luke 2:10

How far did the angels travel in order to announce the news to the shepherds that night. How many hours did it take for them to get to the field where they were watching over their flocks? How was the selection of the spokesangel from heaven's host made?

I don't know enough about angels to be a good speaker. One time, I was asked by a woman how much I knew about angels. I replied that I didn't know much about angels. I was able to get a copy of her book on angels and a bill the next day.

My suspicion is that real angels don't look very much like the ceramic ones found in gift shops. The shepherds wouldn't have been scared if a bunch of tiny cherubs showed up and announced their birth on their tiny harps.

We see glimpses of angels in the Bible that are fast and strong. They are warriors. They are also hit men. They act as guides and saviors for their human subjects. They are also messengers. The message they carry is the etymology for angel.

As we make our pilgrimage to Bethlehem I will be looking deeper into the words of the angels to the shepherds. We can start our journey by taking a closer look to Luke 2's familiar words.

The angel first said, "Don't be afraid." This is the usual opening line for angels when they meet with people, particularly people who are receiving good news from God via their angelic messenger. These words

tell me two things.
This confirms my earlier assertion that real angels are bigger and scarier then the ones depicted on calendars and coffee mugs.
They may appear to be ordinary people, but they could be celestial beings from the other world. How else could Abraham and we be able to entertain angels? However, I believe shock and awe are the most common human reactions to an encounter with an angel.
It is good to know that the word of God through these powerful messengers wasn't a threat but an announcement for good news. God's character and divine purpose for us is positive and positive. Respectful fear of the Lord that encourages us to listen and obey him is not the same as the terror that comes to those that rebel against God or defy his authority. We as a race deserve to be scared when God or one his messengers arrive on the scene. But the main message of angelic announcements is "Fear Not."
Have you ever reacted to something new or unfamiliar with fear? Are you averse to something that turns out to be a blessing instead of a curse?

December 11

And the angel said to them, "Fear not, for behold, I bring you good news of great joy that will be for all the people." - Luke 2:10

The angel then said, "I bring to you great news of great joy!" Sometimes, news and good don't seem to go together very well. There is a war in this area, and a threat to you health over there. Terror alert raised, fire out of control, once-popular public figure disgraced in scandal. It almost feels like a threat when the announcer states, "We'll be having more news after that message."

The angel had great news, and it was going to bring much joy. The winged correspondent announced the birth of the Savior to his audience. He was telling them their greatest problem would be solved and that their worst fears would be overcome. The long-awaited, long-awaited one was here. The announcement was not understood by the shepherds, who I doubt were theologically grounded enough. I doubt you or I could grasp the whole meaning. The angel conveyed the message so that the shepherds understood it. It was good news, not bad news.

The result of hearing the news was great joy. Although their initial reaction was fear, the shepherds soon found joy after they listened and acted upon what they heard. As they returned to their fields to tend their flocks, their joyful praises to God rang out throughout the night.

Is joy overflowing our response to God's word messages? When they hear or read God's word, some people are more sad than joyful. They hear only the condemnation of loss and ignore the message about the Savior. They might be conditioned by guilt to only hear the bad news about God and their relationship with Him. Perhaps pride is unable to accept the possibility of a Savior and so takes offense

At the suggestion that one has not been provided. External factors could also play a role, like prolonged exposure to preaching which condemns by tone and content, but lacks hope-inspiring good information. This teaching can drain the listeners of joy and leave them feeling hopeless.

Although I'm not an angel I can be a preacher. It's probably time to take a walk on the beach or in the woods and reflect about it for a while. Does the word of God I'm called upon to share come across as good news or bad news? Are there signs of joy in the hearts of my listeners? An old preacher once said that the best steak would be rejected if it was wrapped in filthy paper. It's possible, and even common, to convey the best news of Jesus Christ in distasteful language, hateful attitudes, and poor teaching methods. People lose the joy of the gospel when they hear it or read it in this way.

The gospel of a Savior is a message of salvation. I don't suggest that you ignore the sin problem. Faithful preaching is about rebuking and convicting others of their sins. As a preacher, it is important to tell the whole story. Jesus Christ came to Earth, lived a perfect and sinless life, and then died to pay for our sins. God's power raised Jesus from the dead and offers that power to us as well for our lives

Let's not forget these things when we Christmas Pilgrims share a message of God with a neighbor or friend. Let's offer them hope. Let's share the hope of great joy with them.

Consider a time when you were blessed with good news. What was the best part?

What was your reaction to hearing it?

December 12

And the angel said to them, "Fear not, for behold, I bring you good news of great joy that will be for all the people." - Luke 2:10

The angel stated that the joyous good news was for all people. This makes this message different from other types of news. Investors love news about rising interest, but borrowers don't like it. Rainy weather is good news to farmers and their fields. However, it's bad news for those who plan big outdoor events at the same. Even the sports page can bring joy to those on the winning team and disappointment to those who are wearing the colors of the losers.

This announcement was good news for everyone. Everyone needs a Savior. The Savior is here. All people can hear the message of his saving work. It is possible for everyone to be blessed by it. Only those who reject God's offer to save their souls are not blessed.

It is thrilling to consider the universality of the gospel's message. As a Christmas Pilgrim, however, I must see myself in this picture. So do you. This news from angels doesn't only concern the birth of the Savior of the World. It is first and foremost about the birth of your Savior. The angel said, "A Savior was born to you today." This does not refer to the original text being singular or plural. Pilgrims, I ask you to personally believe that this universally good news is for you.

Every day, I receive mail that has been addressed to me by a machine. My name and address were associated with the bill or catalogue by a computer database. It was printed on the label or envelope by a mechanical device. Local postal workers may have sorted the mail into my mailbox as the first human touch. Sometimes, I receive an envelope addressed by hand. Someone wrote me personally and took pen in hand.

This is the kind of mail that I rarely receive.

Open first

This is the email equivalent. It sends email from family, friends, and associates to your Inbox. You will be looking at these emails. The rest of the emails go to Spam, and may not be read at all.

The gospel is a special type of universal. Although it is for everyone, the gospel is specifically addressed to you. Its life-changing, joy-producing good news is for every person. Do not get lost in the crowd or feel like you don't belong. Don't say, "You don't know what I have done or what's been done." I do. God does. He sent Jesus Christ to be your personal Savior. When you see the manger in Bethlehem, you will realize how incredible it is.

What should you do about mail addressed to the Box Holder or Occupant What do you do with correspondence that is sent to your mailbox from a friend? What is the difference?

The Shepherds

December 13

And in the same region there were shepherds out in the field, keeping watch over their flock by night. - Luke 2:8

The campout was an adventure for the younger ones. The older men understood that it was hard work, punctuated with restless periods of trying to sleep on uneven ground. Although it was rare for shepherds to go outside, they did so only a few times per year. There was no doubt about where the shepherds from the suburbs of Jerusalem would spend their evenings when the ewes were bringing in their offspring and when they were carrying their young.

Being outdoors alone, away from the city, had its perks. On cloudless nights, when the air was still and cool, the starry night spectacle was spectacular. The stars shined brighter than diamonds on velvet black, and were more beautiful than diamonds. The night sky was easy for children to recognize and name. There were also those rare, peaceful days when the temperature was not too high, predators weren't attacking, and the pasture was adequate for sheep to graze happily.

Irony was the theme of this night's conversation around the fire in an open field close to Bethlehem. One young man laughed, "They need us," but "they don't want us there."

It was true. The work of shepherds was a significant part of the local economy. The village's lowest workers viewed shepherds as dirty, undesirable, dishonest, and marginalized. The legal proceedings at the city's gate did not permit shepherds to testify. They were considered outcasts and excluded from the main stream of culture because of their occupation.

It was so kind of God to send angels to bring the best news Jewish society and the world could ever hear, to a bunch outcast shepherds. "Unto

You are born this day in the city David a Savior who is Christ the Lord." The ostracized were invited to meet and adore the newborn Messiah.

The terror subsided and the shepherds ran to Bethlehem to answer the angels' call to see the King. They told everyone they met about their incredible night after they found Joseph, Mary, and baby Jesus. Everybody was amazed at the testimony of these shepherds, who were not considered fit to testify. The things they heard and saw changed the hearts of the shepherds who answered the call to be Christmas Pilgrims. They were still shepherds. They were required to return to their flocks to do their work. Their social status had not changed. Their hearts were full of joy and worship as they returned to the fields with their flocks. Mary said that God had shown favor to the humble estate of his servants.
We must remember that the angels didn't appear in Herod's throne or temple courts. They became outcasts in the field, doing work that separated them from the respectable companies. They were despised by their society but God praised them. Christmas Pilgrims, like you and I, should find hope in the story of the shepherds.
Pilgrim, do you ever feel like an outsider? Like you don't belong or aren't valued? The story of the shepherds teaches us a valuable lesson about God.

December 14

When the angels went away from them into heaven, the shepherds said to one another, "Let us go over to Bethlehem and see this thing that has happened, which the Lord has made known to us." And they went with haste and found Mary and Joseph, and the baby lying in a manger. And when they saw it, they made known the saying that had been told them concerning this child. And all who heard it wondered at what the shepherds told them. - Luke 2:15-18

These pilgrims, who smelled like sheep, may have some lessons for us. People who hear positive news should act on it. They raced to Bethlehem to find out for themselves what the angels had said. They followed the instructions on how to find Jesus and Mary, as well as Joseph. They set out to experience it for themselves. They saw and then they told others.

Followers of Christ must not only be aware of God, but also worship him. They are responsible for communicating the good news to others. People who heard the report of the shepherds were stunned by the information they received. The wonderment that their report caused in their listeners was likely due to the wide-eyed enthusiasm of the shepherds.

If church seems boring, it could be because we aren't connecting with our target audience. It's possible that we are comfortable with the way we tell it, because it is familiar to us. We may need to rethink how we communicate the gospel to our society. Is the gospel really what we are "going" to? Are we following Paul's example, who claimed he was all things to all people in order to save some souls? Do we feel the same contagious joy as the shepherds as we share our story as we move and tell it?

Many who had the opportunity to see and hear Jesus in person were disillusioned. This will likely be the case when we share the good news of today. This does not mean that we should stop sharing the good news.

Our responsibility to follow Jesus' instructions to tell others about him does not negate it. Jesus' story of the sower didn't produce any results in the places where the seed fell. Some of the seed did land on the right ground, and it produced the crop. When we do the same as these shepherds, our joy and God's glory are multiplied. And when others hear the good news and are blessed by it.

Are you able to recall the person who shared with you the good news of Jesus Christ? Was there anything that impressed you about their story and the people they served?

Did you ever recommend a restaurant or movie that you liked? You don't know why I asked you that question.

December 15

And the shepherds returned, glorifying and praising God for all they had heard and seen, as it had been told them. - Luke 2:20

People heard the news about the birth of the baby from people who were similar to those who would be receiving him as a child and start his ministry. Jesus would be rejected by the orthodox, but he would be accepted by the outcasts. The priests would mock, accuse, and snub the Galilean, while the common people would happily listen to him.

The angels announced that the good news was for all people. Pilgrim, this would include you as well. They said that a Savior had been born. It should make a difference in whatever place you are in, no matter how hopeless or beaten. Our sins have made us all separate from God, and that is the worst problem. We are lost, and need a Savior who will save us from our sins. This is the message Christmas Pilgrims are invited hear and to receive.

It's important to remember that Jesus Christ was born when we feel abandoned and unloved. Sometimes you may feel like you should borrow a line from David, the baby's ancestor, and scream, "No one cares about my life!" But the message is clear to both shepherds and you: "I care." Angels convey the message of love from God to you.

It is significant that the shepherds heard and saw that night in Bethlehem inspired worship. They returned to the fields, glorifying God and praising Him for all they had seen and heard. This is what makes worship so boring and hollow. We are less likely to worship God if we don't appreciate the good things He has done for us. Worship flows from

Thankful hearts. Our natural reaction should be to give thanks and praise God for what He does. Perhaps we have lost sight of Jesus' wonder and the amazing power of God.

The message sent by the angels to shepherds is also a message expressing assurance. God holds to every promise he makes. For centuries, the promises and prophecies have been building up. Israel's rebellion and faithlessness had brought about hard times for the chosen people. It seemed that God had abandoned them, and that his promises were empty. The miraculous birth of Jesus in Bethlehem was a powerful reminder for the remnant of Israel of God's faithfulness to all his promises.

Luke concludes the story of the shepherds by saying that they saw and heard exactly what they were told when they went to Jesus's. Later, the disciples would discover that Jesus had indeed promised them exactly what he meant. These days, there is a lot of confusion and doubt about the truth. It would be great if there was some certainty in the midst of all this uncertainty. When politicians and advertisers make outrageous promises that insult our intelligence, we aren't sure who to believe. Perhaps you have been hurt by the lies of people you trusted, and you have developed a strong shell of doubt and skepticism in defense. I pray for you and me to have the grace to believe God's promises. I'm confident that God will show us that everything always works out exactly as God has promised, on this journey to Bethlehem and on all of our other journeys.

What shepherd's blessing do you most need right now? Do you need to see God clearly in your worship? Do you need to be more confident? Do you need to remind your broken heart that God loves and knows you?

◆◆◆

The Magi

December 16

Now after Jesus was born in Bethlehem of Judea in the days of Herod the king, behold, wise men from the east came to Jerusalem. - Matthew 2:1

Melchior's mind was racing through the star charts. What was he missing out on? It appeared so suddenly. It was never charted before.

After his part in the king's birthday celebration was over, he ran back to his quarters. He didn't ask anyone why he chose to live on the lower floors of the building. He was unable to walk up the stairs without pain, so it took him a while to get up there. Only one apartment had a balcony that allowed him to see the night sky from the outside.

In two hours it would be dark. He might want to rest, as the night ahead was long. He knew from the moment he lay his head on it that he would not sleep. He was back up within a few minutes, looking at the drawings again. They were highly prized because they had more detail and accuracy than the rest. His charts didn't give any clues about the rogue.

He cancelled all of his appointments for the night after another night of wonder and frustration. Gaspar was contacted by a messenger who called him to arrange a conference. Balthasar was also notified by him, who used the code word in both messages to summon his respected associates without hesitation or question. The others were so excited about the task at hand that they skipped the formalities of meetings when they arrived. Gaspar was still holding onto his scrolls. Balthasar carried the bag that contained their funds.

Melchior asked Gaspar "What did your find?" He hoped that Gaspar would be able explain this strange occurrence using a reference from a sacred text. Gaspar's eyes lit up as he pulled one of the oldest rolls out.

Gaspar stated, "I might have something here." "Look." He gently and masterfully unrolled the parchment with his hands. His finger landed just above the passage.

Melchior's robe dangled behind him as he moved around the table, trying to find the old words. These were words from a prophet named Balaam, according to his research partner. Balaam, though the prediction is found in Hebrew Scriptures was not a prophet of the Hebrew God, but a Gentile who was employed by Balak, the king of Moab to curse his enemy Israel. The prediction was made during a humorous incident in which Yahweh continued to transform Balaam's attempts at cursing Israel into blessings.

It's in the Hebrew Scriptures. It seems to work. Gaspar thought aloud that it was true.
Balthasar laughed, "Israel hasn't been a true player for centuries now."
"But the old stories are quite convincing. Perhaps there is something more to the story.
Prophecies are after all," stated Gaspar.

Their minds were forming an idea, a suggestion that was beyond their current reasoning. They stepped out onto the balcony, looking up at the sky. It was obvious. Melchior exclaimed, "Israel calls this coming King Messiah." Is the star his calling cards? Gaspar and Melchior looked to Balthasar as their treasurer.

Balthasar told them that the journey would be long and difficult. Balthasar realized that their analysis would not stop them from pursuing this idea. They were drawn by the star's bright beam. They were drawn by its magnetism. They were ready to take the road.

Nobody knows the identity of the wise men or whereabouts they came from. What do you think they were like?

(Note: Michael Card's book The Promise has influenced my thinking about the Magi.

December 17

"Where is he who has been born king of the Jews? For we saw his star when it rose and have come to worship him." - Matthew 2:2

The name of the Magi, or wise men, is not as mysterious as it sounds. They were also Christmas Pilgrims. Journalism students are taught to ask questions such as "Who, What, When, Where, Why and How?". It would be difficult for them to write even a single paragraph about the people who came to Bethlehem in order to see a newborn King.

The first 12 verses in Matthew chapter 2 contain all the details about the Magi. The rest of their history is based on legend, tradition, and speculation. Some sources give their names as Melchior, Gaspar or Balthasar. Others tell us they were Persian astronomer-astrologers. We don't know if the gifts indicate that there were three wisemen, but it is possible.

Matthew gives us the date and time Jesus was born during Herod's reign. Even though we don't know where they went, we do know the destination. A star guided them to the area and to the exact spot where Jesus was. We now know the why. They said it in their own words, "We have come here to worship the King Of The Jews." Now we can answer the how. They presented gifts and bowed. How did they know?

In the New Testament, the writer of Hebrews began his book saying that God speaks at different times and in various ways. His communication was through prophets' words and dramatic actions. He also used a mysterious hand to write on a wall. God also sent instructions and invitations to seekers at least once through a mysterious star.

Hebrews' writer also stated that God spoke to them in the last days.

His Son is our salvation. All the Old Testament prophets and methods of

God were pointing to the One through whom we hear God's voice today

--Jesus. Are you familiar with the story of Jesus' transfiguration. Peter, James, and John witnessed Jesus speaking with Moses and Elijah. They heard God speak to them, saying, "This my beloved Son, with which I am well pleased; listen!" We listen to the one that the wise men followed to find.

These Christmas Pilgrims are well known from Christmas pageants and nativity scenes. Any nativity set worth its salt will have wise men, regardless of whether they're made from life-sized plastic figures or delicately hand-painted porcelain for the coffee table. Ironically, some of the most well-known characters from the manger scene weren't even there. Matthew reports that the wise men arrived later than expected, possibly as late as two years later. They did arrive. They traveled a long distance, brought expensive gifts, and kneeled down to worship King Jesus.

The wise men could have felt so proud of their deep knowledge of ancient mysteries, and their potential position as advisors for powerful kings, that they would not have thought to make such a trip. God somehow got their attention. They left behind pride and power and came to worship the promised One in humility.

For some, knowledge can be a bridge between worship and God's presence. But for others, it can be a barrier. Is that possible? What is it that you feel? What is the difference?

◆◆◆

December 18

"I see him, but not now; I behold him, but not near: a star shall come out of Jacob, and a scepter shall rise out of Israel;" - Numbers 24:17

It's interesting that God used a visible sign (the rogue star) and a centuries- old prophecy (from a rogue prophet) to call these pilgrims to Bethlehem. Old Balaam is mentioned in five Old Testament books and three times in the New Testament, but never in a positive light. How odd that his words would be the ones that called them across the miles and centuries: "I see him, but not now; I behold him, but not near. A star will come out of Jacob; a scepter will rise out of Israel."

This reminds us that God comes to us and calls us where we are. That is of course ultimately true in Jesus coming into the world to become like us to save us. We hear it when Jesus tells fishermen that he will make them fishers of men. What better way to reach these scholars of ancient religion and astronomy than to tie an old writing to a new star?

God's willingness to do that is amazing to me. But the wise men's willingness to give up on incantation and knowledge and to follow the star is amazing and instructive, too. They were willing to follow the light they had (quite literally), and it led them to worship King Jesus. That explains why these Gentiles from who knows where came a long way to Bethlehem to worship, while the Jewish religious leaders just down the road in Jerusalem did not.

I would never discount what you know in urging you to make this pilgrimage. I don't know how God might use your background and experience to draw you to himself, but I do not doubt that he will do it. The issue is willingness. Are we willing to listen? Are we willing to follow? Are we willing to humble ourselves, and be genuine seekers?

Pilgrim, are you a long way from acknowledging Jesus as King in your life and heart? Will it cost you a lot to do so? Will it mean that you have to give up things you've long known and practiced? My prayer about this is that God will grant us the grace to remember these pilgrims who followed the star, and walk in their steps. We don't call them "wise men" for nothing.

The Magi followed the "light" they had—the star. Would you have followed such a sign? Are you content to follow the "light" you have—the Bible?

Herod

December 19

When Herod the king heard this, he was troubled, and all Jerusalem with him. - Matthew 2:3

Not everyone was filled with joy when news of Jesus' birth began to circulate. The shepherds rejoiced when they heard the news of a newborn Savior. But King Herod was troubled when he heard from the wise men about a baby who had been born whom they described as "king of the Jews." Instead of elation and relief, Herod felt threatened and angry.

History tells us that the Herods were ruthless despots. Although they were vassals, really no more than hand puppets who served at the pleasure and for the convenience of Rome, they fiercely protected their turf. That may be why Herod was troubled. It certainly explains the murder of all the little boys less than two years old. The Herods killed their own family members if those brothers or children were perceived to be threats. They would not hesitate to slaughter innocent children for the same reason.

Rather than just shaking our heads at the cruelty, let's take a closer look at why Herod was troubled to make sure our own reaction to the good news about Jesus is altogether joyful. You see, Herod probably reacted as he did because he felt the newborn King was a threat to his own throne and crown. You and I know from reading the rest of the story that Jesus' kingdom would not be of this world. It would not be a political, territorial entity, but an all- encompassing spiritual kingdom. But Herod didn't know that. The popular idea about Messiah was that he would restore David's throne and throw off the evil oppressors of the Jews. Even the closest disciples fantasized about their places in the glorious new kingdom. When Herod heard the word "king," he felt threatened. Do you?

Jesus described his control of the hearts, minds and lives of his disciples as "the kingdom of God." Jesus is Lord as well as Savior, and those who follow him must deny themselves to do so. That means we give up on being our own king, and bow down to Jesus as ruler of our lives. It is precisely here that many of us balk. Church is fine, and we realize that we are actually blessed when people around us do what Jesus wants them to do. But we feel threatened when our will is challenged by his will. It is not easy to pray what Jesus prayed in Gethsemane: "Not my will, but yours be done."

It breaks my heart to realize that I have the potential within me to resist and reject the kingship of Jesus just as Herod did. But it's true. Every act of willful disobedience to God in our lives demonstrates to some degree the resistance that Herod felt. You know what I mean, Pilgrim?

We worship Jesus as King. We sing songs about his crown, his throne, his kingdom. How do our daily lives and moment-to-moment decisions test our

December 20

And he sent them to Bethlehem, saying, "Go and search diligently for the child, and when you have found him, bring me word, that I too may come and worship him." - Matthew 2:8

Herod told the wise men to tell him when they found Jesus so that he too could "come and worship" the baby king. Is our worship tainted with a similar hypocrisy when we sing about Jesus being King while clinging to the illusion that we control our own lives? We may say Amen to the prayers at church that praise God as the great King of the universe. But do we at other times stake our claim on the Judea of our hearts and defy his rightful reign over us? Are these uncomfortable questions? I do not mean to be insulting. But these are questions we may need to ask ourselves.

As Christmas Pilgrims, we have a decision to make. We dare not go to Bethlehem as mere curiosity-seekers. We shouldn't be making the journey simply because it is seasonally or culturally expedient to do so. We cannot go to the manger and treat the baby we find there as if he were an offering at a cafeteria: "Oh, the Savior is really appealing. I'll take that, but I think I'll pass on that Lordship." And we must admit that it is possible to go on the journey, to go through the motions, and it all be a sham—no more real than Herod's pretense of worship.

Remember that the Herods were not really kings, not really in control, but simply instruments of Roman imperialism. Ironically, the Herods weren't really Jews either. They were Idumeans, installed on the throne at Jerusalem by the Romans. Old Herod was altogether an imposter as king of the Jews. And Pilgrim, you and I are imposters when we think we're in control! The territory of our hearts is not rightfully ours; we're not actually in control.

The wise men's gifts were expensive, truly fit for a king. But the greatest gifts we could bring to King Jesus are our unconditional surrender of self and genuine worship from our heart. Those precious commodities cost us more than gold, frankincense and myrrh. Giving ourselves to Jesus is an extravagant gift, since it takes all we have and all we are to truly give it. And isn't it wonderful that the only thing we really have to give that we can call our own is exactly what honors Jesus most when we give it to him?

Think about "Your kingdom come, Your will be done" from the Lord's Prayer. Focus on your own heart and life as you pray those words.

Jesus

December 21

And at the end of eight days, when he was circumcised, he was called Jesus, the name given by the angel before he was conceived in the womb. - Luke 2:21

Somewhere in our stuff, probably in a box of old photographs, there is a page of names that we considered before our first child was born. It was 1982, over a year before I would buy my first real computer, so the list is typewritten. I remember the night we sat in my basement office and said the names aloud. I typed a dozen or more possibilities, both boy's names and girl's names. (It was 1982. We didn't know in advance the sex of our firstborn.) Even when she was born, we were still undecided about her full name until she was about three days old. We stared at the blank for the name on the birth certificate a couple of days before committing. But when we came home from the hospital, she was Heather Suzanne McElroy.

Mary knew her baby would be a boy and knew his name would be Jesus before she was even pregnant. She had no pregnancy test, 4-D ultrasound image or baby name book. But she knew because the angel said so. When Joseph came and reported the collaborating message he received from the angel, she knew. Later, after the baby had been born, the delay until the eighth day was a formality of the Jewish circumcision ritual, not the inability of young parents to make a choice about something as important as a child's name.

He was called by more than one name in the prophecies—Wonderful Counselor, Mighty God, Everlasting Father, Prince of Peace, Immanuel to name a few. Each emphasized some aspect of his character, nature or mission. But when the angel told Joseph the name that would be spoken when it was time for ancient Israel's equivalent of the birth certificate, that name was Jesus.

Do you know the meaning of your name? Do you know the story of how your parents chose your name? Does it have some family significance?

December 22

"She will bear a son, and you shall call his name Jesus, for he will save his people from their sins." - Matthew 1:21

When the baby born at Bethlehem was named Jesus, the shadow of the cross was in that name. Although Yeshua was a common name among the Jews, this savior would be the Savior in the ultimate sense of the word. He would save his people out of a fallen world from the guilt, dominion and punishment of sin. He would lay down his life so his saved ones could live without fear of death. He is the Christ, God's anointed. He is Lord of all, and all will confess that truth someday whether we've done so in this world or not. But grateful hearts who know him as Savior love to praise him by his given name—Jesus.

I understand how the baby in the manger that we Christmas Pilgrims long to see may be more appealing than the gruesome execution scene of the man on the cross. But the manger is the necessary prelude to the cross. The One who would die for human beings had to take our form and nature to do so. And the cross was the necessary conclusion of the manger story if God's plan for redeeming us was to be realized. The guilt of sin required a death. We are glad to know that Immanuel (God with us) was born. That message gives us hope. By his life and words, we gain wisdom and guidance for our lives. We can do better than we've done by listening to him and imitating him. The birth of Jesus gives us joy and hope. But it's his death that deals with our sins.

Jesus accepted our punishment in our place. Those who trust in his death and believe in his resurrection can know why they named him Jesus, Savior.

The angels were predicting the cross when they told Mary and Joseph to name the baby Jesus. When the angels told the shepherds that a Savior had been born, they were predicting the cross more than thirty years in advance.

On our way to Bethlehem, we must mix our joy at his birth with the somber realization that his name looks ahead to his death. Many Jews died on crosses in the time of Jesus. But only one was the Savior, born to die for you and me.

The manger and the cross are like bookends on the story of Jesus' life in flesh. Take a while to think about what his birth and his death mean to you. Take a moment and thank him for dying on the cross for you.

December 23

And when the time came for their purification according to the Law of Moses, the brought him up to Jerusalem, to present him to the Lord…
- Luke 2:22

Our pilgrimage to Bethlehem now takes a side trip. Just 41 days after Jesus' birth and six miles up the road from the little town where he was born, we find baby Jesus, Mary and Joseph at the temple in Jerusalem. Luke's description gives more evidence of how deeply devout Mary and Joseph were.

The young parents were following the ancient instructions about the redemption of the firstborn and the ritual of purification following childbirth. In the shadow of the first Passover on the eve of the Exodus from Egypt, God told Moses that all the firstborn among the people and animals of Israel belonged to Him. He later exchanged the 22,000 Levites for the 22,273 firstborn counted in the census ordered a little over a year after the Exodus. Each of the firstborn in excess of the number of the Levites would be redeemed for the price of five shekels (about two ounces) of silver. All the faithful of Israel through the generations observed this custom. Luke does not mention the coins, but does tell us that "they went to Jerusalem to present him to the Lord," an echo of the texts that called for the redemption of the firstborn.

Does Luke also quietly inform us of the young couple's economic status? Back in Leviticus, the Lord told the Israelites to bring a lamb for a burnt offering and a pigeon or turtledove for a sin offering for the atonement ceremony. But if the family could not afford a lamb, two birds would be acceptable. Is Luke saying Mary and Joseph were poor when they brought a pair of turtledoves? Later in life, Jesus frankly told professing followers that he had no home of his own. He looked for breakfast on fig trees and had only
one garment to his name at the time of his death.

In a world that measures greatness and significance by dollars and possessions, Jesus does not seem to measure up. This is a lesson I need to hear as Christmas approaches. We think about spending enough, giving enough and maybe even getting enough. We buy and give and get and accumulate, all in the name of the one who said that life does not consist in the abundance of possessions. I do not want to dampen your holiday spirit. But I need to be reminded (and maybe you do, too) that Jesus came and did without what this world thinks is valuable. And he did it for us. A half- century after the events described by Luke, Paul would use Jesus' poverty to motivate generosity among his disciples: "For you know the grace of our Lord Jesus Christ, that though he was rich, yet for your sake he became poor, so that you by his poverty might become rich."

We admire Mary and Joseph's devotion to the Law and its customs. We're thankful to know that the boy Jesus grew up in a family that respected the word of God. But surely there is more for us to see in this report of their obedience. I think it's significant that the baby at the center of this picture is the one who came because the whole nation (not just the firstborn) needed to be redeemed, and not just the nation, but also the whole fallen race. The human family needed a purification that could be foreshadowed, but not accomplished by the sacrifice of animals. "It is impossible for the blood of bulls and goats to take away sins." As part of his identification with us, our Lord himself became a baby to be redeemed, born of a mother with whom he went through the purification ritual. And then, when he went to the cross, he himself became the redemption price. His blood became the real and effective purifying sacrifice for our sins. We Christmas Pilgrims find yet another reason to bow down and worship. It's not only about how far Jesus came. It's also about how far he would go.

Can you think of a way to remind yourself and your family that Christmas is about much more than the gifts that are exchanged?

Please pause and meditate for a while about the wonder of Jesus humbling himself to become a baby, going through the ritual of redemption and purification, and then ultimately becoming the sacrifice to redeem and purify you.

◆◆◆

December 24

And she gave birth to her firstborn son and wrapped him in swaddling cloths and laid him in a manger, because there was no place for them in the inn. - Luke 2:7

We never took long vacations when I was a boy. My father worked hard, long hours every day. But we would sometimes go to the Gulf Coast for two or three days during the summer.

Back then, we never had reservations in advance. Part of the vacation ritual was going from motel to motel, looking for a room in a place that would be acceptable. In my mind, more than fifty years later, I can still see the signs in front of the motels. The word "Vacancy" was painted on the sign, just like the name of the place. The signs might have white or blue or green neon tubing outlining the letters. But the word "NO" was in red neon. The proprietor could switch it on or off depending on how many customers had signed the register that day, or whether or not the person getting out of the car looked like a desirable guest. The sun was going down. I wanted to be on the beach, not riding up and down the road after being in the car all day. I hated the cruel, red "NO" that told me I was not welcome.

Luke explains in one simple line why Jesus was laid in a manger: "because there was no place for them in the inn." Like hotels in college towns on home game weekends, or motels from a simpler time along the beach, Bethlehem's inns were packed, filled with travelers who had come to comply with Rome's decree to register. When Mary and Joseph arrived, they could not find shelter in the inn.

Forget Ramada or Holiday. This inn from Jesus' day was probably not more than a group of open sheds surrounding a common area. I won't describe it as a courtyard because that's probably too dignified a term for it, and it might make you think of yet another modern hotel chain. Forget quaint, charming, cozy and all the other advertising words that describe today's "homes away from home." In reality, the inn itself was probably not as nice as the stables we see in the annual dramas commemorating Jesus' birth. It would get zero stars in the hotel rating guides.

There's a character called the Innkeeper in most Christmas plays, but we don't find one in the gospel narrative. We don't know if Mary and Joseph were rudely turned away by the proprietor, or angrily driven out of the crowded space by the other guests. Maybe they just peeked in the gate, hoping for a corner in the corral where Mary could rest, before realizing that there was no room.

So Mary and Joseph had to improvise. Was Jesus born in a cave under the inn, or in a stable where the animals were kept? Or was he born in the open air? We don't know. What we do know is that there was no room in the inn for newborn Jesus.

What emotions are stirred in you when you read there was no room for Mary and Joseph, and that Jesus' first bassinet was an animal feeding trough? What does Luke's account of this have to do with your life?

You

December 25

He came to his own, and his own people did not receive him. But to all who did receive him, who believed in his name, he gave the right to become children of God, who were born, not of blood nor of the will of the flesh nor of the will of man, but of God. And the Word became flesh and dwelt among us, and we have seen his glory, glory as of the only Son from the Father, full of grace and truth. - John 1:11-1

Pilgrim, you're probably ahead of me on this one, aren't you? You know what I'm going to ask. Do you, my fellow Christmas Pilgrim, have room in your heart and in your life for Jesus? We think it's sad that the Savior of the world had to be born in such a difficult situation. We shake our heads as we imagine the poverty in which he lived his life, remembering how he warned a prospective disciple, "Foxes have holes, and birds of the air have nests, but the Son of Man has nowhere to lay his head." And the lack of accommodation he found in his birth and life was mirrored in the hard- hearted rejection he experienced from the very people he came to save. "He came to his own, and his own people did not receive him."

But do we have room for him in our crowded lives? The innkeeper and other guests could not have known they were turning away the Messiah. Maybe you're like them, and just didn't know. But I know. Maybe you do, too. We know and believe he is "the only Son from the Father, full of grace and truth." Do we still sometimes find no room for Jesus in the inn of our hearts? Our preoccupation with our plans and desires, our ongoing need to acquire more stuff, and the incessant demands of business and family life make it hard for Jesus to find a place, let alone first place in far too many lives.

You might be like my friend, a young, hard-working businessman. He was not making excuses when he told me that he simply did not have time to read
his Bible and pray. I didn't have to tell him how important it was. He knew he should. But from the time he was awakened by the clock in the early morning until he collapsed from exhaustion late in the evening, it

was hard to find room in his day for time with God. Is your day like that? Others have so many things that need to be done every day, or so many activities planned that they simply cannot find room for God.

As Christmas Pilgrims, let's commit to make room for Jesus. We've read this book and thought these thoughts on a purposeful, thirty-day journey together to see Jesus during the Christmas season. We've made it to Christmas. That's good. I commend you for doing it. The real challenge is to make real room for Christ tomorrow, and in the real routine of our daily lives. Most of us live with very little margin. If one part of our plan doesn't happen on time, our tightly scheduled events can topple like falling dominoes. Media outlets constantly inundate us, each clamoring for our attention. We're driven by the desire to acquire. It's hard to concentrate, to carve out time, to make room. It's not always easy to obey, "Be still and know that I am God." But it is important. Taking time to read, think and pray in quietness every day is one of the most important and rewarding commitments a disciple of Jesus can make.

So, it's a day for gift-giving. I believe the most important gift you could give today would be the gift of yourself to the Lord. We owe him far more than just a little time each day or week. I'm talking about surrendering your whole life to Jesus, who came so far to live and die and rise again for you.

Thank you for reading, for sharing this journey with me. Merry Christmas, Pilgrim. I pray that God's inexpressible gift, the gift of his Son, will be yours this Christmas Day, and every day. God bless you!

What comes to your mind when you read the apostle Paul's words calling Jesus God's "inexpressible gift"?

If it's difficult to schedule daily time for Bible reading and prayer in your routine, think of one change you could make that would create some time. Could you implement that change tomorrow? Will you do it? Please say YES, Pilgrim! Then by God's grace stay on the journey with Jesus until you arrive at Home!

◆◆◆

www.ingramcontent.com/pod-product-compliance
Lightning Source LLC
LaVergne TN
LVHW090134160826
845673LV00017B/2469

* 9 7 9 8 7 5 4 9 2 1 1 3 9 *